THE

Dan Quayle

QUIZ BOOK

For People Who Think They Are Smarter Than The Vice-President

Jeremy Solomon and Ken Brady

LITTLE, BROWN AND COMPANY

Boston   Toronto   London

For Louis and Elsbeth Solomon
—J. S.

For Robert O. Shipman and
Lauren Jean Welch
—K. B.

Also by Solomon and Brady
The Wit and Wisdom of George Bush

First Edition

ISBN 0–316–80359–6

10 9 8 7 6 5 4 3 2 1

BP

Published simultaneously in Canada
by Little, Brown & Company (Canada) Limited

Printed in the United States of America

Contents

Acknowledgments

Claudia Weinstein

Walter V. Robinson

Jill Farmer

Nancy Curtis

Maureen Curran

Colleen Mohyde

Kurt Wise

Sally Brickell

Anne Pollock

THE

DAN QUAYLE

QUIZ BOOK

Introduction

WHEN George Bush picked Senator J. Danforth Quayle to be his vice-presidential running mate in 1988, Bush thought he was adding a missing element to the ticket: a young, handsome face, a running mate who, in Bush's words, had "an ability to get votes from women." Quayle also offered impeccable conservative credentials, which ex-moderate Bush needed to shore up his support among the distrustful right wing of the Republican Party. And Quayle, unlike other potential running mates, was not a strong personality and had no national constituency of his own. It was, as William Schneider of the American Enterprise Institute remarked, "the nation's first father and son ticket." Thus George Bush, the Vice-President who raised loyalty to an art form, would not have to worry that his number two might steal the show from him.

Dan Quayle, however, also brought a number of unpleasant surprises to the Bush campaign. Quayle's college record left so much to be desired that Quayle refused to release his grades. In fact, his record was so mediocre that in 1982 the faculty of DePauw University, his alma mater, had voted against giving Senator Quayle an honorary degree — although the vote was overturned by the university's president. And to the embarrassment of many conservatives, Quayle had joined the National Guard in 1969, thereby avoiding the draft. After college he was admitted to the Indiana University School of Law, but under unusual circumstances. A member of one of the wealthiest families in Indiana, Quayle entered the law school through an experimental program for disadvantaged students, a forerunner of the school's affirmative action program. Also, Bush's running mate had a reputation for being more concerned with golf than with politics. As a former Quayle congressional aide noted, "When he saw the first few rays of sunshine, he'd be out on the golf course." Worst of all, Quayle seemed unable to speak coherently in public. At a news conference shortly after joining Bush on the GOP ticket, Quayle made his famous declaration that "I didn't live in this century." A new genre of jokes was born, and protesters began appearing at Quayle campaign stops with signs that read VERY PRETTY, BUT CAN HE TYPE? and CHICKENHAWK. It was not an auspicious start for the new vice-presidential candidate.

After the first rush of negative publicity, however, the Bush campaign staff swung into action. For the rest of the campaign Quayle was allowed to visit only small towns in conservative regions, and personal contact with the national press was nearly eliminated. As a result, Quayle was able to weather the storm and remain on the ticket without endangering the Bush campaign. It was a major feat of political damage control.

Dan Quayle, however, remained Dan Quayle. Once in office, he was permitted to open his mouth again, just a little. What came out invariably made *The Tonight Show,* if not the front page. As the *Wall Street Journal* noted after the election, Quayle "appears on his way to becoming the most lampooned Vice-President in history."

Here, then, as a tribute to the man who makes everyone feel smart, is a quiz book on the life and words of our forty-fourth Vice-President. As a test it is not graded (something Dan would appreciate), but should you want to score your performance, please feel free to do so. Only those who get a perfect score can say they are as intelligent as Quayle — the rest of you are on a higher plane. Good luck. But remember, no cheating.

CHAPTER ONE
The Early Years

AS A YOUTH, Dan Quayle was much different from the Dan Quayle we know today. He was shorter, for one thing. His young friends, who obviously recognized Quayle's leadership potential even then, nicknamed him "Eddie Haskell," after the effusive teenager on *Leave It to Beaver.*

But it was his performance in the classroom that people would remember years later. By most accounts Quayle approached his studies with all the enthusiasm of someone paying a parking ticket. Quayle's former professors and classmates, at least those who remember him, indicate that Quayle tiptoed through college classrooms on tiny cat's feet. However, college did serve two important functions: it supported the golf team and it made fraternity life possible.

Do you know what Quayle was like as a youth? What *did* he learn in college? Try this first part of the quiz to find out.

1. According to his mother, as a child, how did Quayle deal with his problems?

A. "We had an old tomcat named Ned and he would chase it around the house. He never caught Ned but he sure did scare him."

B. "He went to his room and sulked."

C. "We had a chain saw and he would go out back in the woods and cut down trees. By the time he graduated from high school he had cut down the whole woods."

D. "Playing golf he learned how to control himself and to overcome his mistakes."

E. "He would catch flies and tear their wings off."

2. In an interview with the *Wall Street Journal*, Quayle was asked about growing up in Arizona from 1955 to 1963. What was his response?

A. "Growing up in the land of Goldwater I realized that nuclear weapons weren't something to be afraid of."

B. "That's where I learned how to play golf."

C. "When you gaze out over the desert, you realize that out there you can see as far as the eye can see."

D. "I learned about the drive of the Mexican people. They love hard physical labor, and I still think Mexican women make the best housekeepers."

E. "Living in a new part of the country made me aware of just how many states there really are."

3. According to former DePauw University classmate Joseph Wert, what did Quayle major in in college?

A. "Girls, golf, and alcohol."

B. "Golf, alcohol, and girls."

C. "Alcohol, girls, and golf."

D. "Girls, alcohol, and golf."

E. "Golf, girls, and alcohol."

4. How did former DePauw University classmate Clark Adams remember Quayle?

A. "His idea of a Vietnam protest was to go out with only one date on a Saturday night."

B. "When he sold his books back at the end of the semester, he always got top price because they were still like new."

C. "The only thing I can remember is he was on the golf team and he was quite a ladies' man. This is in 1968. To be politically apathetic in those years was to be a nonentity on campus. He was not a guy to take a position on anything except who his date was on Friday night and where to get drunk on Saturday night."

D. "Whenever we played touch football he had to be the quarterback or he wouldn't play. And then, he'd always call a quarterback sneak."

E. "He was always slapping you on the back. He was friendly and had a nice smile, but he wasn't what you'd call a good student. Actually his slap was more of a punch."

5. How did Quayle, a conservative on defense and national security matters, explain his 1969 decision to join the National Guard?

A. "It was that or go to Canada, and I didn't want to leave Indiana, so I went into the guard."

B. "Well, growing up in Huntington, Indiana, the first thing you think about is education."

C. "There are other ways to serve your country. I was looking at things in the macro sense."

D. "I thought someone with my level of abilities — intelligent and well-educated — could better support the war effort at home."

E. "I was a strong supporter of the war, but I didn't want to get killed."

6. What did Quayle say he learned while in the National Guard?

A. How to make sloppy joes

B. How to shine shoes

C. How to weld

D. How to read

E. How to use a lawn mower

7. Shortly before he was released from the National Guard in 1975, Quayle took a written exam that tested him in such areas as "fundamentals of writing" and "Army information." The average test score was 75. What did Quayle score?

A. 96

B. 86

C. 76

D. 66

E. 56

8. How did Quayle respond when asked about the ethics of his admission to Indiana University Law School under a special program for disadvantaged students?

A. "My mom and dad just made a phone call to the president of the university. There's nothing wrong with that."

B. "I *was* disadvantaged."

C. "When the admissions committee learned about my military record, they decided I deserved a chance."

D. "As my grandmother once told me: 'It's a doggy dog world out there and you've got to wag your tail harder than the rest if you want to make it.'"

E. "I deserve respect for the things I did not do."

9. According to a former co-worker, what were Quayle's duties when he worked at the Indiana Attorney General's office?

A. Coordinating the work of the assistant attorneys general

B. Photocopying

C. Researching dog bite cases

D. Watering the plants

E. Climbing the ladder to get the really big books off the top shelf

10. The résumé Quayle gave to the Bush campaign stated that Quayle had been chief investigator of the Indiana Attorney General's consumer office for two years. How long had Quayle headed the office?

A. Two hours

B. Two days

C. Two weeks

D. Two months

E. He never headed the office.

CHAPTER TWO
On the Hill

AFTER HIS academic triumphs, his successful defense of Indiana against the Vietcong menace, and his rapid ascent in the field of family-owned newspapers, Quayle was ready for a new challenge. He found this in politics.

He ran for a congressional seat in 1976, and, surprising everyone except himself, he won. The House of Representatives proved to be everything Quayle had hoped: it had its own gym. However, it was not all fun and games. Occasionally he was expected to vote on a bill or attend a committee meeting.

In 1980 he pulled off a stunning upset of incumbent Birch Bayh to win a seat in the Senate. There he thrived by using debating techniques perfected by irate motorists on busy city streets. But Dan Quayle's legislative legacy is a matter of public record and we are all familiar with it. Or are we?

11. In 1976, when asked by an Indiana GOP county chairman to run for Congress, what was Quayle's response?

A. "Congress is for sissies."

B. "That's the big one in Washington, right?"

C. "Why would anyone vote for me?"

D. "What are the [golf] courses like down there?"

E. "I'll have to check with my dad."

12. According to an Indiana reporter, in 1976 when Quayle first announced he would run for Congress, what was the reaction of the local press?

A. Reporters "laughed when Quayle rose to speak and asked him if it wasn't past his bedtime."

B. Reporters "joked with Quayle that his family would buy Fort Wayne to win the election for him."

C. Reporters "were angry with Quayle for holding the Fort Wayne press conference in a building without a bathroom."

D. Reporters and Quayle "went out for beers and played 'quarters' at a Fort Wayne bar after the press conference."

E. Reporters "ran out of his Fort Wayne press conference to cover a breaking police story."

13. During a strategy session for his first congressional campaign, what did one of Quayle's supporters suggest he run as?

A. "Dan Quayle, draft dodger"

B. "Dan Quayle, not just for breakfast anymore"

C. "Dan Quayle, student"

D. "Dan Quayle, Hoosier"

E. "Dan Quayle, neighbor"

14. True or false: When Quayle started out in politics, he was so impressionable that people who knew him said that he was "a victim of his last conversation."

15. During his two terms in the House of Representatives, where did Quayle's attendance record on floor votes and committee meetings rank among the Indiana delegation?

A. First

B. Second

C. Fourth

D. Seventh

E. Last

16. How did a top Quayle congressional aide describe Quayle's two terms in the House of Representatives?

A. "His greatest improvement probably came in his putting. The country clubs around D.C. have some of the best greens in the country."

B. "He was always on the phone. But not with congressional matters, with the weather recording, dial-a-joke, things like that."

C. "Dan had two TV's in his office. He would watch reruns of *Gilligan's Island* and *Hogan's Heroes* at the same time."

D. "His attendance record was lousy. They didn't know where he was a lot of the time. He'd be in the gym or he'd sneak off to play golf and they'd have to call all around to find him."

E. "He was like a kid in a candy shop. He kept introducing bill after bill after bill. Of course, they never went anywhere, and eventually the leadership told him to stop it."

17. In a 1980 Indiana Senate campaign debate with incumbent Senator Birch Bayh, Quayle argued with Bayh over the Constitution. What did Quayle say?

A. "The Constitution of the United States proves the old saying, that paper is mightier than the sword. The sword might be sharper but the paper is the stronger of the two in a fair fight."

B. "The Boston Tea party hasn't been forgotten, and that's what the Constitution says to me, Senator, and that's what we disagree on. If you think you can forget the high taxes and Jimmy Carter mentality that gave birth to the greatest Constitution the world will ever see, you can rest assured that you're on the wrong side of the tracks."

C. "Some of the Democrats have this idea, this idea, that they know what the thoughts were inside of the men who signed that Constitution of ours, but don't be fooled at what you have heard them or Senator Bayh say because they only said it."

D. "The Constitution, as you well know, being the constitutional authority that you have been over the years on the Judiciary Committee, knows in the Constitution that the Congress creates the federal courts."

E. "In Washington there is a little room where they maintain our Constitution and I want to make sure we don't forget that and enter a period where we may never see her again. That's a big difference between you and I, Senator, I believe the Constitution is here to stay and should be, and you don't and that's all I'm going to say on this issue."

18. In the 1980 debate with Senator Birch Bayh, after blaming incumbents such as Bayh for the country's problems, Quayle was asked whether he was also part of the problem since he had served four years in the House of Representatives. How did Quayle respond?

A. "Absolutely not. I am not part of the problem. I happen to be a Republican."

B. "Where'd you get that idea? Look at me, do I look like I'm part of the problem?"

C. "If you compare the record, the real record, then you'll see that I have never had any problems, not one. That's what makes him part of the problem and not me."

D. "No. No. No. Do you hear me? No."

E. "I think the voters of this great Hoosier state can recognize that I am and always will be a Hoosier first, and a part of the Washington taxocracy second."

19. In 1986, as a member of the Senate Armed Services Committee, what did Quayle have to say about inefficiency and corruption in Pentagon weapons procurement?

A. "I think when you start all this talk about $400 hammers and $600 toilet seats, you're missing the real issues, which is how much bang for our buck are we getting. And I think we're getting a pretty good bang."

B. "In the past we have tried too much to prevent the making of mistakes."

C. "I make a pretty good watchdog, woof-woof. No one better try anything when I'm guarding the henhouse."

D. "We may have our problems, but I know that Napoleon would have given his left arm for just one Midgetman missile."

E. "Guns and weapons cost money. Some people don't realize that. And without oversimplifying, lots of guns and weapons cost lots of money. But we get it all back in the freedoms we enjoy."

20. True or false: While in the Senate, Quayle tried to persuade Merriam-Webster's dictionary to change the definition of "Hoosier" to "Someone who is quick, smart, a winner, unique, and brilliant."

21. What was Quayle's major legislative accomplishment as Senator?

A. The Really Neat Training Partnership Act

B. The Welders Training Partnership Act

C. The Job Training Partnership Act

D. The Grain Training Partnership Act

E. The Training Bra Partnership Act

22. In 1987, Senator Quayle introduced a special tax break for what group?

A. Golf pros

B. Performance artists

C. People with blond hair and blue eyes

D. Welders

E. Indiana senators

23. How did Quayle try to persuade Kansas Senator Nancy Kassebaum to vote for the confirmation of Reagan judicial nominee Daniel Manion?

A. By jumping up and down on the Senate floor and shouting at her

B. By offering to give her golf lessons

C. By sending a Strip-o-Gram to her Senate office

D. By bending her arm behind her back

E. By offering to buy her a drink after the vote

24. According to Quayle, what is the difference between the House of Representatives and the Senate?

A. "They don't call you kiddo in the House, like they do in the Senate."

B. "I never really noticed."

C. "You can get a bunch of guys and go down to the gym and play basketball. You can't do that in the Senate."

D. "There are lots more people in the House. I don't know how many exactly — I never counted — but at least a couple hundred."

E. "In the Senate I'm one of only two Hoosiers. In the House there were a bunch of us."

CHAPTER THREE
The Candidate

MOST people first glimpsed Dan Quayle in August 1988 when George Bush announced his selection of Quayle as his running mate. Quayle, enthusiastic as a game-show contestant, joined Bush on stage in a typical burst of energy.

But questions about his background soon began to trouble the campaign. The decision to insulate Quayle from the media paid off, although trying to hide Dan Quayle completely was like trying to hide an elephant under a bushel basket.

No matter how much his handlers tried to control and rehearse him, Quayle etched his unique signature on the campaign of 1988. How much do you remember about Dan Quayle and the campaign trail? Find out as the quiz continues.

25. Before announcing his choice of Quayle as his running mate, what comment did Bush make?

A. "I'll be out at the appropriate time to make that announcement and it will be laden with suspense . . . and everyone will say, 'What a fantastic choice.'"

B. "Oh, the running mate thing."

C. "We've been throwing a lot of names in the hamper . . . and it's just a matter of seeing which ones float."

D. "I'm looking for someone who looks good on television and who's willing to play second fiddle to a guy like me . there aren't that many around, you realize."

E. "It's the process of elimination. And as of now we've eliminated just about everybody . . . which is pretty much what we expected to happen."

26. At the Republican rally in August 1988 in New Orleans when Bush announced Quayle as his running mate, what did Quayle do when he joined Bush on stage?

A. He giggled uncontrollably and had to leave the stage for three minutes to calm down.

B. He hit Bush in the stomach and cried, "Let's go get 'em!"

C. He wrapped Bush in a headlock and gave him noogies.

D. He kissed Bush on the lips and said, "I love George Bush and I love America!"

E. He froze in front of the crowd and stuttered, "I *am* old enough to be Vice-President."

27. After George Bush selected Quayle as his running mate, Barbara Bush kissed Quayle on the cheek. How did Quayle respond?

A. He rubbed his cheek.

B. He patted her on the behind.

C. He blushed.

D. He punched her in the arm.

E. He turned the other cheek.

28. What were Quayle's first words to the GOP convention in his acceptance speech?

A. "Ask not what your country club can do for you, ask what you can do for your country club."

B. "Hi, Mom."

C. "I can see we're going to have a lot of fun in this campaign."

D. "How-de-e-e-e!"

E. "Can I take these balloons home for my kids?"

29. At a 1988 campaign rally in Jackson, Tennessee, Bush made this statement with Quayle standing at his side.

A. "Who is this twerp, and why is he smiling all the time?"

B. "We cannot gamble with inexperience in that Oval Office."

C. "I mean, gosh, it's not like he's some kid fresh out of a Cub Scout troop. He's a United States Senator — and he's a Hoosier!"

D. "I'd like to present to you the next President of the United States."

E. "He's taken a licking, but he keeps on ticking."

30. Five weeks after voting against a bill that would elevate the Veterans Administration to a cabinet-level agency, how did Quayle defend his negative vote at an August 1988 campaign rally?

A. "Five weeks is a long time. I can't remember the vote. There are so many, you know."

B. "Marilyn told me to."

C. "A youthful indiscretion."

D. "I thought it was a vote for 'veterinarians.'"

E. "Had I known I would be running for Vice-President, I assure you I would have voted differently."

31. In a 1988 campaign speech, Quayle expressed pleasure at serving on the ticket of _____.

A. "George Butch"

B. "George the bush"

C. "George McGovern"

D. "George Butt"

E. "George the weenie"

32. During a heated exchange with reporters in 1988, Quayle said he would accept only yes or no questions. Which question did Quayle refuse to answer because it was "not a yes or no question"?

A. Had his wife taken the Indiana bar exam for him?

B. Had he offered to take his name off the ticket?

C. Had he refused to release his college transcript because he had been caught cheating?

D. Had he told a reporter that he thought Camp David was a Jewish summer camp outside of Washington?

E. Had he taken illegal drugs in college?

33. During the 1988 campaign, how did Quayle explain his statement that "rural Americans are real Americans"?

A. "Rural Americans *are* real Americans. There's no doubt about that. You can't always be sure with other Americans. Not all of them are real."

B. "I'm a rural, and I'm an American. That's what makes me real. See?"

C. "It's rural America. It's where I came from. We always refer to ourselves as real America. Rural America, real America, real, real America."

D. "I just meant that rural Americans are real. So are urban Americans. They are real too. We are all real. Really."

E. "The really rural Americans are really, really rural. Real. Rural. Rrrrrr. I like words that begin with *r*."

34. During the 1988 campaign, why did GOP staff workers read Quayle gaffes out loud at staff meetings?

A. Because Marilyn made them

B. So Quayle could learn from his mistakes

C. To demonstrate how unfair the media was being to Quayle

D. For laughs

E. To convince themselves that Quayle was actually running

35. During the 1988 campaign Quayle refused to answer questions about his parents' involvement in the John Birch Society, saying the matter was irrelevant. When reporters asked him why this information was not relevant, how did Quayle respond?

A. "That all happened a long time ago, before this century."

B. "My parents had nothing to do with me."

C. "These stories are nothing more than attempts at character association."

D. "I had no control over my parents before I was born."

E. "Because I said so."

36. During the 1988 campaign, what commercial slogan did Quayle use to describe the Bush/Quayle ticket?

A. "Everything you always wanted in a President and less."

B. "The heartbeat of America."

C. "The quicker picker-upper."

D. "Reach out and touch someone."

E. "Not just for breakfast anymore."

37. How did Quayle respond to a farmer's question concerning local agriculture at a campaign stop in Missouri?

A. "Whatever you guys want, I'm for."

B. "Farmers are the breadbasket of the American economy."

C. "Serious questions deserve serious answers, so I'll have to pass on that one."

D. "I'm a Hoosier, and if there's one thing us Hoosiers understand it's who butters our bread."

E. "Farming is a way of life, but it's also a way of growing things."

38. In Fort Smith, Arkansas, a reporter asked Quayle if he would model his vice-presidency after that of any other Vice-President. How did Quayle respond?

A. "George Bush, of course. He stands for what it means to be number two."

B. "Models are for kids."

C. "Well, if Winston Churchill had been Vice-President, I would model my vice-presidency on what his would have been like."

D. "I can assure you that my vice-presidency will be unlike any other."

E. "I don't know if there's one that comes to mind."

39. What time was it when Quayle said "good night" to a Miami audience during the 1988 campaign?

A. 8:00 A.M.

B. 10:00 A.M.

C. Noon

D. 2:00 P.M.

E. 4:00 P.M.

40. On the 1988 campaign trail Quayle spoke of "precise _____."

A. precipitation

B. Presbyterians

C. precision

D. pretzels

E. predictions

41. True or false: Robert Redford introduced himself at a Dukakis rally with the words, "Hello, everybody. I'm Dan Quayle."

42. What did Quayle say to his debate advisor, Roger Ailes, as Quayle practiced hand gestures before the vice-presidential debate?

A. "Should I keep my head down and my left arm straight?"

B. "How about if I make an arm-wrestling-type move toward Bentsen? It might scare him."

C. "Should I make some shadow figures with my hands? Wanna see my doggy? Woof-woof."

D. "Hey, Roger ... does ... on, on this, you know, if I'm gonna, if I, if I decide on my gesture over there ... is that all right ... you don't mind?"

E. "What do I do if Bentsen gives me the finger when no one's looking?"

43. What accessory did Representative Dennis Eckart use when he played Quayle in debate rehearsals with Senator Lloyd Bentsen?

A. A golf tee to stick behind his ear

B. A whoopee cushion

C. A Dan Quayle hand puppet

D. A pogo stick

E. A map that showed Indiana as the largest state in the Union

44. During the vice-presidential debate, what did Quayle say he would do if he unexpectedly became President?

A. Go on national television and tell the American people that their worst fears had been realized

B. Call Marilyn and ask her what to do next

C. Try to retake the moon from the Russians

D. Change the locks on the White House

E. Say a prayer and call a cabinet meeting

45. How did Quayle defend his vice-presidential debate answer to the question, "What would you do if you had to assume the duties of the presidency?"

A. "I meant I would pray that George Bush was in heaven and I would have a cabinet meeting to find out what to do next."

B. "They didn't give me any hints."

C. "I had not had that question before."

D. "My underwear was too tight and I couldn't concentrate."

E. "That was a trick question."

46. When Lloyd Bentsen said his famous "you're no Jack Kennedy" line in the vice-presidential debate, how many times did Quayle's Adam's apple bob?

A. Once

B. Twice

C. Nine times

D. Forty-seven times

E. It didn't bob. Quayle has no Adam's apple.

47. During the vice-presidential debate, what did Quayle say after Lloyd Bentsen complained that he couldn't hear the questioner?

A. "That should come out of his time."

B. "Jack Kennedy wasn't hard of hearing."

C. "He's not supposed to say that."

D. "I can hear you OK."

E. "Little trouble with the hearing aid, huh, gramps?"

48. Speaking at a campaign rally in Eau Claire, Wisconsin, Quayle said that he and Bush were interested in _____.

A. "that cute blonde up in the fifth row"

B. "making America great again after eight years of failure in the White House"

C. "not much of anything"

D. "your erogenous zones"

E. "the human infrastructure"

49. What did Quayle say at a garden center and produce market in Baltimore?

A. "When you see a shopping mall like this one that I'm standing on right now, you realize the unquenchable spirit that flows through each and every American's vein. Without that spirit, these toys and other things would never find their way to the boys and girls that they need so badly."

B. "Let me tell you something. As we were walking around in the store, Marilyn and I were just really impressed by all the novelties and the different types of little things that you could get for Christmas. And all the people that would help you, they were dressed up in things that said 'I believe in Santa Claus.' And the only thing that I could think is that I believe in George Bush."

C. "How many of us just stop to smell the tomatoes or onions. I haven't had much time to do that in a place like this and neither has Marilyn for a while. So you can bet that when we have the time we'll be heading for some neat places like this to make our noses do the walking. But the campaign has some smells in it that I couldn't describe to you even if I wanted to."

D. "Flowers are a lot like a political campaign. You start with something small — a seed or an idea — then take care of it. And if there's enough light and sun and water and rain, you get something that's bigger than the thing you started. Of course, the more fertilizer you spread around the better off you are."

E. "I push the cart and Marilyn tells me where to push. The produce section is so colorful, like a movie or something. I want to come back because when you're on the road all the time, like we've been, it's nice to just stop and shop and go to a great place like this one, where there are things all displayed so beautifully that anyone could buy them."

50. In an interview with CBS anchor Dan Rather, vice-presidential candidate Quayle denied having had sex with lobbyist Paula Parkinson. What was unusual about his comment?

A. It was true.

B. Rather had photographs of Quayle and Parkinson playing miniature golf.

C. Rather had not asked about the incident.

D. Quayle had referred to her as "honey."

E. Quayle had given a different answer to NBC anchor Tom Brokaw.

51. What activity does Quayle traditionally undertake on the day of an election?

A. He has lunch with Jack Lord.

B. He dresses up in a bunny suit and harasses voters at the polls.

C. He buys a pair of suspenders.

D. He goes to the dentist.

E. He listens to his Alvin and the Chipmunks record.

CHAPTER FOUR
The
Vice-President

CONTRARY to popular belief, a Vice-President does more than go to funerals — though no one seems to know what that means. There are strong hints that Dan Quayle might know, but he is not telling. Since his inauguration in January 1989, Quayle has worked hard to project the image of a serious statesman. Reports emanate from the White House that Quayle is studying diligently and that he has become a valuable member of the Bush administration. Yet even though he is now Vice-President, Dan Quayle has not changed significantly. By now you know quite a bit about Quayle as a youth, as a member of Congress, and as a national candidate, but how much do you know about him as Vice-President?

52. After the 1988 election, Quayle told reporters, "I'm going to be involved." When reporters asked what he was going to do for the rest of the day, what was Quayle's response?

A. "Listen to my Jack Kennedy tapes."

B. "Not a whole lot."

C. "Read Plato's *Republic.*"

D. "Attend a real estate seminar."

E. "Have lunch with George Bush."

53. After the 1988 election, how did Quayle explain that he would be more careful with his words?

A. "The minute I stop talking, that's when you'll hear something."

B. "Shorter sentences. Shorter sentences. Shorter sentences."

C. "From now on you won't hear me answer any question, even if it's in Chinese."

D. "I've got to stop shooting up my mouth."

E. "Verbosity leads to unclear, inarticulate things."

54. What did Quayle say after the swearing-in ceremony on Inauguration Day?

A. "My feet hurt, and I'm hungry."

B. "I was standing behind Barbara Bush and I couldn't see everything that was going on. But I know that it was quite a spectacle."

C. "This just goes to prove that in America anybody can become Vice-President."

D. "You've got to have a dream. And today my dream has become your dream. We are all in a dream today."

E. "They asked me to go in front of the Reagans. I'm not used to going in front of President Reagan, so we went out behind the Bushes."

55. How did the new Vice-President respond when asked what he thought he might not be good at in his new job?

A. "Could you repeat the question?"

B. "Lots of things, but I don't know what they are yet. When I get to them, then I'll know."

C. "Funerals. Dead people are a bummer."

D. "I'm certain there are things that I will encounter in which I could improve, and once I encounter those things, I'm sure that I will take specific steps to improve in those specific things."

E. "I can't think of anything."

56. What event is on Vice-President Quayle's schedule every week?

A. Really, really important meetings with really, really important people

B. A foot massage

C. Lunch with George Bush

D. Spaghettios for breakfast with his children

E. Drum practice

57. Speaking to a Nashville luncheon of the United Negro College Fund, the Vice-President attempted to invoke the group's well-known slogan, "A mind is a terrible thing to waste." What did he say?

A. "What a waste it is to lose one's mind. Or not to have a mind."

B. "My mind is a terrible thing."

C. "Time is a terrible thing to waste. So let's get the show on the road."

D. "There is a lot of waste in our minds. This bears reminding."

E. "The blind are a terrible thing to waste. They deserve equal opportunity."

58. At a party for his forty-second birthday, what did the Vice-President do when asked to make a wish before blowing the candles out on his birthday cake?

A. He jumped up and down and screamed, "I want a *chocolate* cake."

B. He shook his head and said, "I can't think of any."

C. He pouted because the pony hadn't shown up yet.

D. He growled and pointed a knife at the throat of PBS reporter Judy Woodruff.

E. He sucked the helium out of a balloon, and, imitating a Munchkin from *The Wizard of Oz,* sang "Happy Birthday."

59. When he first meets a man, Quayle has a habit of doing what?

A. Embracing the man and giving him a kiss

B. Repeating the man's name five or six times in an effort to memorize it

C. Vigorously shaking the man's hand and punching him in the arm

D. Giving the man a high-five

E. Stomping on the man's toes with the heel of his shoes

60. What were the Vice-President's first words when he called Secretary of Transportation Samuel Skinner to invite him to the Indianapolis 500?

A. "Hey, Sammy baby, how about seeing some *real* transportation?"

B. "Vr-r-o-o-m, vr-r-o-o-m, vr-r-o-o-m."

C. "Bet my car goes faster than your car."

D. "Hello, this is Mario Andretti. Is Al Unser there?"

E. "Turbo-charged action. The screaming howl of cars out of control. The smell of sweat, beer, and burning rubber."

61. What did the Vice-President say when he received an honorary degree at the historically black Fisk University?

A. Fisk has "turned the corner, because it wasn't long ago that I wouldn't have been admitted to this college."

B. Fisk has "honored someone who doesn't deserve it."

C. Fisk has "the most black faces I have ever seen."

D. Fisk has made "the greatest comeback since Bill Cosby returned to network television."

E. Fisk has "recognized that there have been many great black Americans, starting with Martin Luther King."

CHAPTER FIVE
Domestic Issues

WHEN IT COMES to his positions on domestic issues, Dan Quayle knows what he knows. A traditional conservative, he speaks often of families, friends, and neighbors. He sees many of the country's social ills as caused by a breakdown of traditional values. Despite his strong convictions, Quayle does not always say what he means. But does he know what he means to say? Usually. The question is, do you know what he means? Continue the quiz to find out.

62. Speaking to a group of farmers, Quayle said the 1988 farm bill was a good one. When someone asked him what his message for farmers was, what was his response?

A. "Where's the beef?"

B. "Farmers are the buttocks of this country."

C. "My message?"

D. "Sow your seed for the future, vote for George Bush and Dan Quayle."

E. "You're the heartburn of America."

63. Quayle said that government could help the homeless by _____.

A. keeping interest rates low

B. selling them land in the national parks

C. giving them their own two feet to stand on

D. keeping the streets cleaner

E. eliminating the Department of Housing and Urban Development

64. How did Quayle describe the Republican Party's position on the family?

A. "The GOP has a warm feeling for families. I have one and I'd like to have more."

B. "Republicans know that children are an important by-product of reproduction."

C. "Republicans understand the importance of the bondage between parent and child."

D. "Members of this party all came from families. And that's a lot more than you can say about the other party."

E. "The GOP has never been pro-family. We know that without them we aren't going to survive."

65. At the Missouri State Fair in Sedalia, Quayle was asked to explain agricultural target prices. What was his response?

A. "Farmers make the food we eat. Uh. All of us, uh, all of us who eat depend on their hard labor for the food we eat. You can't sit down at a restaurant without a farmer. I know this. The Hoosier state is full of farmers. They grow things. I know this because I'm from Indiana."

B. "Target practice? I, uh, don't do much shooting. Uh, I, uh, play golf. George Bush likes to hunt, and he's a life member of the National Rifle Association. Uh, target practice is something that's important to me because I'm from Indiana. And Hoosiers know that it's, uh, important to know how to shoot a gun."

C. "Target prices? Uh. How that works? I know quite a bit about farm policy. I come from Indiana, which is a farm state. Deficiency payments — which are the key — that is what gets money into the farmer's hands. We got loan, uh, rates, we got target, uh, prices, uh, I have worked very closely with my senior colleague, Dick Lugar, making sure that the farmers of Indiana are taken care of and, uh, we have spent a great deal of time on farm issues."

D. "There's a very simple way to explain that. Suppose, uh, you have a target — a goal — you want to achieve it. That's the target price. Then you make it profitable for farms to hit that goal or target, whichever it may be. You do this by allowing, uh, the market place to 'target' its own goals or, uh, prices. That's generally how that works. Of course, when this breaks down, uh, you've got a less-than-ideal situation."

E. "That's when you, uh, target prices. It's the bull's-eye approach. Get the ones in the middle. That way farmers — I come from an agricultural state — get their fair share. They should too. Because, uh, farmers are the backstroke of this country. Uh, I mean backbone."

66. According to a 1987 *Gary Post-Tribune* editorial, Quayle deserved credit for protesting government subsidies of what industry?

A. The honey industry

B. The cat litter industry

C. The newspaper industry

D. The maraschino cherry industry

E. The tattoo industry

67. Discussing education, Quayle said, "We're going to have the best-educated American people _____."

A. in a really long time

B. over my dead body

C. or I'll eat those words

D. in the world

E. for the cost of a tank of gas

68. In the 1988 campaign, Quayle was criticized by veterans' groups for missing a key 1987 vote to provide funding for homeless veterans. Why did Quayle miss this vote?

A. He was on a skiing vacation with a Playboy bunny.

B. He didn't believe there were any homeless veterans.

C. He was giving a speech to a National Guard convention.

D. Marilyn had grounded him.

E. He was playing in a golf tournament.

CHAPTER SIX
A Man of the World

AS vice-president, Dan Quayle has had the opportunity to travel the globe and speak to citizens of many foreign countries—Indonesia, Australia, El Salvador, Hawaii. He has shown an instinctive knack for communicating with people of other lands and for adapting to local customs, like showing up two hours late for a meeting with the vice-president of Indonesia and pronouncing "Pago Pago" as "Pogo Pogo" while speaking there. So make sure your papers are in order, check your baggage, and let us tag along with our guide Dan Quayle, man of the world.

69. How did the Vice-President address a group of Samoans gathered to greet him when he visited American Samoa?

A. "Aloha! Boy, am I glad to be in Hawaii!"

B. "How. Me represent great white chief in Washington."

C. "You all look like happy campers to me. Happy campers you are, happy campers you have been, and, as far as I am concerned, happy campers you will always be."

D. "Surf's up!"

E. "I'm here to talk about my Job Training Partnership Program."

70. How has Quayle described the Holocaust?

A. "A tragedy of epidemic proportions."

B. "It was the best of times, it was the worst of times."

C. "An obscene period in our nation's history."

D. "A typical example of Nazi expressionism."

E. "Regrettable, but inevitable."

71. What argument did Quayle use to defend funding for the Star Wars antisatellite weapon system?

A. He said they look pretty when they blast off.

B. He referred to Tom Clancy's novel *Red Storm Rising,* in which antisatellite weapons save the United States from a Soviet nuclear attack.

C. He said the program would create jobs for unemployed aerospace engineers.

D. Because he said so.

E. He said the program would also help in the war on drugs.

72. Before leaving Washington for a 1989 trip to Central America, Quayle said the U.S. _____ violence in El Salvador.

A. "concedes"

B. "celebrates"

C. "calculates"

D. "condones"

E. "collects"

73. Once he arrived in El Salvador, Quayle told journalists that the U.S. would _____

A. "restore human rice. I mean rights."

B. "help El Salvador become the wholesome and fun kind of place that kids and grandparents like to visit, like Florida."

C. "work toward the elimination of human rights."

D. "push El Salvador to get its house orders. I mean its house in order."

E. "begin bombing in five minutes."

74. True or false: At a 1989 Belgian Embassy reception in Washington, Quayle remarked that "I was recently on a tour of Latin America and the only regret I have was that I didn't study Latin harder in school so I could converse with those people."

75. In May 1989, what did Quayle note about the condition of the world?

A. "I believe we are on an irreversible trend toward more freedom and democracy — but that could change."

B. "It's politics as usual. World politics with a capital *W*."

C. "The world is round, like an egg. And it's a key factor in the world today."

D. "The hills are alive with the sound of freedom."

E. "I like to think of that Beatles song 'Please Believe Me' ['Please Please Me'] when I think of the world. Because if you don't believe, then what have you got?"

76. During a visit to Hawaii, how did the Vice-President describe the Aloha state?

A. "Hawaii has always been a very pivotal role in the Pacific. It is *in* the Pacific. It is a part of the United States that is an island that is right here."

B. "This is a beautiful country, *and* the people speak English."

C. "If *Jack Lord* lives here, it's OK by me."

D. "Hawaii is *actually* more of a peninsula than an island."

E. "You are a people made of molten rock. Formed *in* the fire, you are a fiery people, people who are full of spirit and fire. Fire — one of the ancient four elements of air, water, fire, and, uh, land. That's what makes you so great."

77. Why was the Vice-President almost two hours late for an official meeting in Jakarta with Indonesian Vice-President Sudharmono?

A. He was late leaving a tour of an Australian brewery.

B. He and Marilyn insisted on going for an extra swim and then playing another game of tennis before leaving an Australian luxury resort for the Indonesian capital.

C. He stopped on his way to see the movie *Ferris Bueller's Day Off*.

D. He hadn't read his briefing books, and Quayle's aides insisted that Air Force Two circle the Jakarta airport for an hour and a half while Quayle finished his reading.

E. He insisted that Air Force Two make an unscheduled stop at Surabaya, location of the only McDonald's in Indonesia.

78. En route to Venezuela, what did the Vice-President do to brush up on Venezuelan politics?

A. He asked Marilyn if there was anything "tricky" he should be aware of.

B. He played with a Mexican jumping bean.

C. He asked if he could ride up front with the pilots as they approached Venezuela.

D. He slept through the entire flight.

E. He phoned former President Richard Nixon for advice.

CHAPTER SEVEN
Marilyn

MARILYN QUAYLE has always taken more than a casual interest in her husband's career. When Dan was a member of Congress, she worked as an unpaid aide. During the campaign of 1988 she was intimately involved in the decision-making process. More than once, she was the person who abruptly cut off press conferences when she felt questions were becoming too challenging.

Yet Marilyn is more than an extension of her husband. In many ways she is more interesting and more complex than Dan. She too is a lawyer, and friends and former classmates describe her as intelligent and hardworking.

Marilyn Quayle obviously sets high standards, and she expects her husband to live up to them. How much do you know about Marilyn Quayle?

79. As a girl, what was Marilyn Quayle's nickname?

A. "Rasputin"

B. "Marilyn"

C. "Fido"

D. "Pocahontas"

E. "Merit"

80. What organization did Marilyn found while in college at Purdue?

A. Brunettes for Nixon

B. Future Second Ladies of America

C. The Pep Girls

D. The Olive Oyl Look-alike Club

E. Future Housewives of Purdue

81. How has Marilyn Quayle described her first impression of Dan?

A. "I swooned when he told me of his dream for the Job Training Partnership Act."

B. "We both knew it that first night. Everything just clicked perfectly."

C. "He spilled a milkshake on my dress at the drive-in."

D. "He said he'd respect me in the morning — and he did."

E. "He wanted to ride around the park in a horse-drawn carriage. But since there weren't any in Indianapolis, he made horsey noises all night."

82. How has Marilyn Quayle described her role during Quayle's first congressional campaign?

A. "A day didn't go by when he didn't forget something, and I had to drive to the office and bring it to him."

B. "I made all the decisions."

C. "I made him a brown bag lunch every day, and it always had a Twinkie in it. Dan loves them."

D. "I did my best to keep him off the links."

E. "I wouldn't let him watch *Hogan's Heroes.*"

83. When asked about allegations that her husband had had an affair with lobbyist Paula Parkinson during a golf vacation in Florida, how did Marilyn Quayle respond?

A. "Let me tell you, anyone who knows Dan Quayle and what Dan Quayle is like at a golf course knows that if there's a golf course around, that's all he's going to look at."

B. "I know he was good because I had him followed."

C. "Do you believe everything you hear? This is rumormongering pure and simple. You in the media have nothing better to do than tear our family apart. You ought to be ashamed of yourself."

D. "We have an open marriage, so what he does on his trips is his business. He doesn't ask me what I do when he's at the office."

E. "Dan wouldn't dare."

84. True or false: Marilyn Quayle's personal cause is disaster preparedness.

85. How did Marilyn Quayle describe her husband?

A. "A sex machine"

B. "A great Hoosier"

C. "A studious sort"

D. "One of a kind"

E. "An artist deep inside"

86. How did Marilyn Quayle respond to suggestions that she is smarter than her husband?

A. "Tell me something I don't already know."

B. "I'm getting really tired of hearing about how smart I am and how dumb Dan is. Would you be happier if I dyed my hair blond and wore a push-up bra?"

C. "I think that obviously I would have not married Dan Quayle had I not thought he was an equal to me."

D. "It's not cast in stone that a husband has to be smarter than his wife."

E. "I didn't marry him for his brains."

CHAPTER EIGHT
Friends and Enemies

EVERYONE has an opinion about Dan Quayle. Ever since Bush chose Quayle to be his running mate, headline writers and political pundits have been having a field day. For example, during the 1988 campaign, the *New Republic* described the Bush/Quayle ticket as "999 points of light, and one dim bulb."

People who love Quayle — his immediate family, for instance — adore him, and people who do not love him are not shy about making their opinions known. The criticisms of Quayle, especially those that suggest he may not be very bright, have forced Quayle's supporters — his immediate family, for instance — to come to his defense. Yet often these words of praise sound more like backhanded compliments. Read through the following comments from a range of observers, and try to pick the correct answers. Then make up your own mind.

87. According to John Palffy, Quayle's former Senate staff economist, what can Quayle's life be reduced to?

A. "Blue eyes, blue blood, and a rich daddy"

B. "Reverse evolution"

C. "Family, golf, and politics"

D. "A passionate concern for the working men and women of America"

E. "Divine intervention"

88. During the 1988 campaign, Theodore Bendall, a longtime Quayle friend and family attorney, said that if he could change one thing about Quayle, it would be to _____

A. "get him to stop fidgeting. He still can't sit still for more than five seconds."

B. "increase his IQ. He is not an intellect."

C. "make him slow down. He's just a dynamo, and sometimes I worry about him."

D. "get him to quit watching television. He is addicted."

E. "get him to quit speaking off the cuff. He sounds as dumb as an ox when he does."

89. How did a congressional colleague from Indiana describe Quayle?

A. "Worth his weight in fool's gold."

B. "He's personable, he's handsome, he's fun to be around, and he's about a quarter of an inch deep."

C. "A remarkable chip shot."

D. "He is amazing. After you meet him you wonder, seriously wonder, *how* he got elected."

E. "He does some of the craziest things in elevators."

90. What did conservative activist Richard Viguerie say about the Bush staff's attitude toward Quayle after the election?

A. "They're building the space station for him."

B. "They think he was born to be Vice-President."

C. "They'd like to put him under house arrest at Burning Tree or Congressional [two Washington area country clubs]."

D. "They're thinking about cutting back on maintenance for Air Force Two."

E. "They want him to get cable [television]."

91. After being accused of overly aggressive rhetoric in the style of former Vice President Spiro Agnew, Quayle asked Bush, "Do you think that I'm becoming like Spiro Agnew?" What was Bush's response?

A. "Dan, I knew Spiro Agnew. Spiro Agnew was a friend of mine — and you're no Spiro Agnew."

B. "Dan, we are all different. Spiro Agnew was Spiro Agnew. You're you, and nobody — not even you — can change that."

C. "If you can accomplish half of what Spiro Agnew did, we'll be in a fine kettle of fish, Dan."

D. "Dan, you're a Chihuahua. Spiro Agnew was a Doberman."

E. "Dan, I picked you because of your ability to say whatever comes into your head. If that's the way Spiro Agnew was, well, so what? Spiro Agnew was a fine Vice-President."

92. Match the Quayle nickname with its source.

A. "Wet Head"	1. Secret Service
B. "Elvis"	2. College
C. "Skippy"	3. Senate
D. "Florida's third Senator"	4. Campaign television crews
E. "Scorecard"	5. House of Representatives
F. "The Q-ster"	6. Senate
G. "Faceman"	7. College
H. "The Tinkertoy Senator"	8. Bush staff

93. Match the statement with the Quayle spectator.

A. "The deer-caught-in-the headlights look"

B. "A well-intentioned but clumsy Saint Bernard puppy"

C. "Behind those big blue eyes there was nothing."

D. "Constitutionally chirpy"

E. "J. Stepford Quayle"

F. "The second or third lead in a spring break movie"

G. "He has the IQ of lunch meat."

H. "One imagines a young Mickey Rooney trying to imitate Franklin Roosevelt."

1. *Boston Globe* reporter Chris Black

2. Arsenio Hall

3. *Esquire* Editor Lee Eisenberg

4. DePauw University English professor William C. Cavanaugh

5. *Time* reporter Allessandra Stanley

6. *New Republic* literary editor Leon Wieseltier

7. *New York* reporter Joe Klein

8. *Washington Post* columnist Tom Shales

I. "He looked more like a startled deer, one who'd been blinded by our high beams."

9. Reagan arms control advisor Kenneth Adelman

CHAPTER NINE
Quayle on Quayle

DAN QUAYLE is a man who knows himself. He is not plagued by any self-doubts concerning his identity, and he is not the type to engage in lengthy soul-searching. Or any soul-searching. Quayle has always been confident of his own abilities and sure of his beliefs, and his confidence is no doubt one reason for his meteoric rise to the top. This trait is most evident when Quayle talks about himself. Dan Quayle has no trouble defining Dan Quayle — he believes in family, God, Hoosiers, George Bush, and the Job Training Partnership Act, and above all he believes in Dan Quayle. If you believe you know Dan Quayle as well as he knows himself, test your knowledge in this final portion of the quiz.

94. In a 1986 conversation about his career, how did Quayle explain his great success at such an early age?

A. "My grandmother always told me, 'If you're going to stand in the garden, don't be a weed.'"

B. "I have complete confidence that whatever I want to do, I can do. I am confident that things will turn out right for me. And they always have."

C. "I know how to analyze issues and people. I acquired this ability playing golf. You have to be able to clear your mind of everything, which I am pretty good at."

D. "I have this drive inside me, and this drive is what has driven me on my long drive to where I am today."

E. "Vitamins. I don't usually admit it, but I take a lot of vitamins. E. C. A. B. And of course Q."

95. During the 1988 campaign, how did Quayle describe himself?

A. "I'm not a yuppie. I'm a Senator."

B. "I'm not the village idiot. I'm a politician."

C. "I'm not a sumo wrestler. I'm a golfer."

D. "I'm not a beekeeper. I'm a defense expert."

E. "I'm not a rocket scientist. I'm a vice-presidential candidate."

96. How does Quayle describe the way he makes a decision?

A. "I narrow it down to two choices and then I flip a coin."

B. "It depends on the type of decision. If it's something like what to have for dinner or what movie to see, I don't put a lot of thought into it. But if it's something big, like an important Senate vote, I'll spend a little more time thinking it through."

C. "I sort of mentally throw a dart."

D. "Depending on the decision, I call my wife or I call my dad. Occasionally I call my eldest son. It just depends."

E. "Some people spend a lot of time thinking, 'Should I do this or should I do that?' I don't. I just decide what I want to do and do it. I don't go over and over decisions. My wife does, but I don't. It's a matter of self-confidence."

97. In an interview with the *Wall Street Journal*, Quayle was asked about his reading habits. What was his response?

A. "Shakespeare, Joyce, and Tolstoy."

B. "I used to."

C. "Ziggy and Beetle Bailey."

D. *"Welders Monthly."*

E. "Only what Marilyn makes me read."

98. In an NBC television interview shortly after the presidential election, how did Quayle describe himself?

A. "A huge question mark."

B. "I know myself like the back of your hand."

C. "Older than a lot of people my age."

D. "Eager to learn, eager to please."

E. "Presidential lumber."

99. What is Quayle's favorite movie?

A. *Being There*

B. *Hoosiers*

C. *The Color Purple*

D. *Caddyshack*

E. *Ferris Bueller's Day Off*

100. Discussing his tendency to mangle his speeches, the Vice-President mused:

A. "Speeches garble I frequently less than before, I think, and you can quote that on me."

B. "*I* know what I mean."

C. "You've got to keep your tongue under lock and key when you're in politics. Mine's under house arrest, but sometimes it gets out and says what it wants to. Then *I* catch heck for it."

D. "As a speaker, I am improving all the time. And as I improve, my speeches get better. As I get better, my improvement goes up. Up. Up. Up."

E. "Every once in a while, you let a word or phrase out and you want to catch it and bring it back. You can't do that. It's gone, gone forever."

Answers

1. D	15. E	30. C
2. B	16. D	31. B
3. A	17. D	32. B
4. C	18. A	33. C
5. B	19. B	34. D
6. C	20. True	35. E
7. E	21. C	36. B
8. E	22. A	37. A
9. B	23. A	38. E
10. D	24. C	(After pausing and looking to an aide, he added that he would pattern himself after George Bush.)
11. E	25. A	
12. E	26. B	
13. C	27. A	
14. True	28. C	
	29. B	

39. B

40. C

41. True

42. D

43. A

44. E

45. C

46. B

47. D

48. E

49. B

50. C

51. D

52. B

53. E

54. E

55. E

56. C

57. A

58. D

59. C

60. B

61. D

62. C

63. A

64. C

65. C

66. A

67. D

68. E

69. C

70. C

71. B

72. D
(Quayle later said he meant "condemns.")

73. C

74. False
(Although rumored to have said this, Quayle in fact did not.)

75. A

76. A

77. B

78. E
(In a 1958 visit Nixon's car had been stoned in Venezuela.)

79. E
(because she won so many honor badges)

80. C

81. B

82. B

83. A

84. True

85. C

86. C

87. C

88. B

89. B

90. C

91. A

92. A. 5
(because he
spent so much
time in the
House gym)

B. 4
(because
sightings of
him were so
rare during the
campaign)

C. 7

D. 6
(because he
frequently
went there to
play golf)

E. 1
(because of his
love for
competitive
sports)

F. 8

G. 2
(because of his
good looks)

H. 3

93. A. 5
B. 1
C. 4
D. 9
E. 8
F. 6
G. 2
H. 7
I. 3

94. B

95. A

96. E

97. B

98. A

99. E

100. E

Notes

1. *New York Times,* Bernard Weinraub, October 31, 1988.
2. *Wall Street Journal,* Tom Bethell, March 31, 1989.
3. *Boston Globe,* Michael Kranish, August 21, 1988.
4. *Boston Globe,* Michael Kranish, August 21, 1988.
5. *Boston Globe,* Chris Black, August 18, 1988.
6. *New York Times,* Bernard Weinraub, October 25, 1988.
7. *Washington Post,* Michael Isikoff and Joe Pichirallo, August 24, 1988.
8. *Manhattan, inc.,* John Seabrook, November 1988, p. 95.
9. *Wall Street Journal,* Jill Abramson and James B. Stewart, September 16 1988.
10. *Boston Globe,* Michael Kranish, August 27, 1988.
11. *Washington Post,* George Lardner, Jr., and Dan Morgan, October 2. 1988.
12. *Fort Wayne News Sentinel,* Mark Helmke, May 15, 1979, as quoted in *The Making of a Senator: Dan Quayle,* Richard F. Fenno, Jr. (Washington: CQ Press, 1989), p. 4.
13. *The Making of a Senator: Dan Quayle,* Richard F. Fenno, Jr. (Washington: CQ Press, 1989), p. 5.
14. *New York Times Magazine,* Maureen Dowd, June 25, 1989, p. 36.
15. *Washington Post,* George Lardner, Jr., and Dan Morgan, October 2, 1988.

16. *The Making of a Senator: Dan Quayle,* Richard F. Fenno, Jr. (Washington: CQ Press, 1989), p. 12.

17. Lake County Senate Debate, Lake County, Indiana, October 17, 1980.

18. Lake County Senate Debate, Lake County, Indiana, October 17, 1980.

19. *Boston Globe,* Michael Kranish, September 28, 1988.

20. *U.S. News & World Report,* Lynn Rosellini, May 29, 1989, p. 26.

21. *The Making of a Senator: Dan Quayle,* Richard F. Fenno, Jr. (Washington: CQ Press, 1989).

22. *National Review,* Cato, September 16, 1988, p. 25.

23. *Time,* Margaret B. Carlson, August 29, 1988, p. 25.

24. *The Making of a Senator: Dan Quayle,* Richard F. Fenno, Jr. (Washington: CQ Press, 1989), p. 18.

25. *Washington Post,* Bill Peterson, July 22, 1988.

26. *The New Yorker,* Elizabeth Drew, September 12, 1988, p. 96.

27. *New York Times,* Maureen Dowd, August 17, 1988.

28. *U.S. News & World Report,* Andy Plattner, August 29, 1988, p. 32.

29. *The New Yorker,* Elizabeth Drew, October 10, 1988, p. 111.

30. *Boston Globe,* Michael Kranish, August 26, 1988.

31. *Los Angeles Times,* John Balzar, October 2, 1988.

32. *Washington Post,* Thomas B. Edsall and Bill Peterson, August 20, 1988.

33. *Wall Street Journal,* Michael McQueen, October 21, 1988.

34. *Newsweek,* Peter Goldman, November 21, 1988, p. 110.

35. *Washington Post,* Myra MacPherson, October 10, 1988.

36. *Boston Globe,* Michael Kranish, October 20, 1988.

37. *Time,* Laurence I. Barrett, September 5, 1988, p. 16.

38. *Los Angeles Times,* Cathleen Decker, October 16, 1988.

39. *Los Angeles Times,* Douglas Jehl, November 2, 1988.

40. *Newsweek,* Douglas Walker, September 5, 1988, p. 34.

41. *Newsweek,* October 10, 1988, p. 21.

42. *Time,* Richard Stengel, October 17, 1988, p. 21.

43. *Time,* Richard Stengel, October 17, 1988, p. 21.

44. *New York Times,* B. Drummond Ayres, Jr., October 11, 1988.

45. *Boston Globe,* Chris Black, October 7, 1988.

46. *U.S. News & World Report,* Michael Kramer, October 17, 1988, p. 37.

47. *Time,* Richard Stengel, October 17, 1988, p. 21.

48. *Washington Post,* Tom Sherwood, October 16, 1988.

49. *Los Angeles Times,* Douglas Jehl, November 6, 1988.

50. *Newsweek,* Peter Goldman, November 21, 1988, p. 108.

51. *Washington Post,* Kent Jenkins, Jr., November 9, 1988.

52. *Scholastic Update,* Steve Manning, January 13, 1989, p. 6.

53. *The Associated Press,* Washington, D.C., December 1, 1988.

54. *New York Daily News,* Bill Bell, January 21, 1989.

55. *New York Times Magazine,* Maureen Dowd, June 25, 1989, p. 34.

56. *Newsweek,* November 28, 1988, p. 39.

57. *New York Daily News,* Knight-Ridder newswire, May 16, 1989.

58. *New York Daily News,* "Applesauce" column, February 24, 1989.

59. *The Making of a Senator: Dan Quayle,* by Richard F. Fenno, Jr. (Washington: CQ Press, 1989), p. 13.

60. *New York Times Magazine,* Maureen Dowd, June 25, 1989, p. 34.

61. *New York Times Magazine,* Maureen Dowd, June 25, 1989, p. 34.

62. *Los Angeles Times,* Bob Secter, August 27, 1988.

63. *Washington Post,* Kent Jenkins, Jr., November 4, 1988.

64. *In These Times,* Maggie Garb, September 27, 1988, p. 5.

65. *Boston Globe,* Michael Kranish, August 26, 1988.

66. *Gary Post-Tribune,* June 3, 1987.

67. *Los Angeles Times,* John Balzar, October 2, 1988.

68. *Boston Globe,* Michael Kranish, August 24, 1988.

69. *Newsweek,* "Perspectives" page, May 8, 1989, p. 13.

70. *The New Yorker,* Elizabeth Drew, October 10, 1988, p. 102.

71. *Newsweek,* Douglas Walker, September 5, 1988, p. 34.

72. *Newsweek,* Eloise Salhoz and Ann McDaniel and Thomas M. DeFrank, February 13, 1989, p. 18.

73. *In These Times,* Joel Bleifuss, March 1, 1989, p. 4.

74. Answer: False

75. *Wall Street Journal,* Ronald G. Shafer, May 26, 1989.

76. *Newsweek,* "Perspectives" page, May 8, 1989, p. 13.

77. *New York Times,* Maureen Dowd, May 8, 1989.

78. *New York Daily News,* David Hinckley, June 20, 1989.

79. *Newsweek,* George Hackett, October 24, 1988, p. 23.

80. *Time,* Alessandra Stanley, January 23, 1989, p. 27.

81. *Newsweek,* George Hackett, October 24, 1988, p. 23.

82. *Time,* Alessandra Stanley, January 23, 1989, p. 27.

83. *Washington Post,* Donnie Radcliffe, August 18, 1988.

84. *U.S. News & World Report,* Lynn Rosellini, May 29, 1989, p. 27.

85. *Newsweek,* George Hackett, October 24, 1989, p. 23.

86. *Washington Post,* Marjorie Williams, October 20, 1988.

87. *Time,* Margaret B. Carlson, August 29, 1988, p. 24.

88. *Boston Globe,* Michael Kranish, August 21, 1988.

89. *The Making of a Senator: Dan Quayle,* Richard F. Fenno, Jr. (Washington: CQ Press, 1989), p. 12.

90. *Newsweek,* George Hackett and Howard Fineman, November 21, 1988, p. 13.

91. *Boston Globe,* Michael Kranish, March 17, 1989.

92. A. *The Making of a Senator: Dan Quayle,* Richard F. Fenno, Jr. (Washington: CQ Press, 1989), p. 12.

    B. *Wall Street Journal,* David Rogers, October 4, 1988.

    C. *U.S. News & World Report,* Andy Plattner, August 29, 1988, p. 32.

    D. *U.S. News & World Report,* Lynn Rosellini, May 29, 1989, p. 26.

E. *New York Times,* Maureen Dowd, May 8, 1989.

F. *U.S. News & World Report,* Andy Plattner, November 21, 1988, p. 26.

G. *Boston Globe,* Michael Kranish, August 21, 1988.

H. *New York Times Magazine,* Maureen Dowd, June 25, 1989, p. 34.

93. A. *Time,* Alessandra Stanley, October 10, 1988, p. 33.

B. *Boston Globe,* Chris Black, September 11, 1988.

C. *Cleveland Plain Dealer,* Keith C. Epstein, August 19, 1988.

D. *Newsweek,* November 28, 1988, p. 39.

E. *Washington Post,* Tom Shales, August 19, 1988.

F. *New York Times Magazine,* Maureen Dowd, June 25, 1989, p. 20.

G. *Arsenio Hall,* April 5, 1988.

H. *New York,* Joe Klein, October 3, 1988, p. 16.

I. *Esquire,* Lee Eisenberg, December 1988, p. 37.

94. *The Making of a Senator: Dan Quayle,* Richard F. Fenno, Jr. (Washington: CQ Press, 1989), p. 6.

95. *Time,* Alessandra Stanley, October 10, 1988, p. 34.

96. *The Making of a Senator: Dan Quayle,* Richard F. Fenno, Jr. (Washington: CQ Press, 1989), p. 45.

97. *Wall Street Journal,* Tom Bethell, March 31, 1989.

98. *Time,* George J. Church, January 30, 1989, p. 27.

99. *New York Times Magazine,* Maureen Dowd, June 25, 1989, p. 20.

100. *U.S. News & World Report,* Lynn Rosellini, May 29, 1989, p. 26.